All About Archie: Bringing Up A Puppy

By Helen Edwards

DISCLAIMER

The information and recommendations in this book are given without any guarantees on behalf of the author, who disclaims any liability with the use of this material.

To my gorgeous boy, Archie x

Contents

INTRODUCTION

Our dog, Archie, came into our lives when he was eight weeks old; he's two now. During the time we've had him, there have been many ups and downs – thankfully, more ups – and now we can't imagine life without our Archie.

It is very hard work though, bringing up a puppy, and no matter how prepared you think you are, if you've never had a puppy or a dog before, you're going to have the shock of your life. Having a dog when you were a child doesn't count, because no doubt your parents did all the hard work, whilst you had all the fun. That was my experience anyway, whilst my husband, Simon, had never had a dog, and was only used to cats.

We didn't rush into things. We researched dog breeds. We read up on life with a dog, and what we'd need for our puppy in the early days, but nothing we read prepared us for the Archie effect.

Puppies bring with them a lot of love; there are all the cuddles, the joy of seeing them romping through the grass like little lambs, and the fact they follow you everywhere. I remember a little nose nudging my ankles whenever Archie followed me into the kitchen, and when we were playing in the lounge he used to dive into my arms and bury his face in the crook of my arm.

There are lots of pluses, obviously, to getting a puppy, but there are a whole host of things you won't have considered, simple things: you won't be able to leave any of your stuff out if you want it to remain intact; lie-ins are cancelled; TV programmes interrupted; not being able to eat in peace … all because there's a little puppy demanding your attention. The daily walk (or walks) take their toll, especially when the weather is bad, and also when your puppy just wants to sniff everything. Walks with Archie can be incredibly boring at times because it's very much a stop-start process.

And then there's all the messy stuff: picking up poos; clearing up diarrhoea and vomit; cleaning your puppy's bottom when he's got poo stuck on it; cleaning your puppy when he's been digging; the constant battle over muddy paws on the carpet; the fact your home looks like a bomb's hit it when your puppy's let loose. These may be the days when you wonder what you've done, when you think you can't do it any more.

Keep plodding on. As your puppy gets older, things **do** get easier. You'll get to know your puppy, and will know what works (or doesn't work) for him. Every dog (and indeed, every owner) is different. This book tells you something of my story and what I've learnt on a trial and error basis. It's aimed at first-time puppy parents, but some of it will be applicable to first time adult dog owners too.

Maybe it won't be such a shock to everyone, getting a puppy for the first time. I'm sure many people will be far more laid back than Simon and I were, but judging by the number of puppies (and dogs) which are given up each year, other people have found bringing up a puppy hard work. No-one wants to be in the position of feeling unable to cope and feeling they have no choice but to give their puppy up, so if reading this book helps you – fantastic!

Love from Helen and Archie x

'On Archie's first day with us it was lovely watching him toddle around the place – weird, too, as for years it had just been the two of us.'

ADVANCE PLANNING

There's no doubt about it, having a pet is expensive. For a puppy, it's not just the obvious things like the initial cost of buying your pup, insurance, food, bedding, collars, leads, toys, and so on. There'll be things you've never thought about, like flea tablets, worming tablets, annual booster vaccinations, shampoo, treats, grooming, and day care. And as they grow, you'll be replacing collars and leads, beds and other equipment. So make sure you factor all that in before you make the final decision to buy a puppy. Can you afford one?

Essential items which I think you'll need to get prior to bringing your puppy home are (in no particular order):

*Basket

*Blanket

*Food and water bowls (choose either ceramic or stainless steel bowls because your puppy will very likely think his plastic bowl is a toy or a chew. Archie used to toss his around, even when there was water in it!)

*Food – check with the breeder what food your puppy is currently eating.

*Toys – suitable for puppies (remove all plastic tags).

*Treats – suitable for the age of your puppy. There are treats for younger puppies, older puppies, and adult dogs. Check the packet or ask a member of staff in the pet shop.

*Poo bags

*Puppy pads

*Wipes

*Towels – your old ones will do.

*Grooming supplies

*Collar and lead – we had to use a cat collar for Archie when he was really small because all the collars for puppies/dogs were too big. Then I moved on to one of the click-style collars, which are much easier to put on a squirming puppy. Nowadays Archie will stand still when I put his collar on.

*A collar with your contact details on it (or a dog tag) – a legal requirement in the UK.

*Some antibacterial disinfectant spray for those accidents on the carpet (check it's suitable for use in homes with pets – I'd buy one from a pet shop).

*Sometimes a puppy pack will be given to you by the breeder, containing food, a blanket, and so on, so again ask them about that.

*A travel crate to bring pup home in, which you can later use at home to help with toilet-training. The crate should be big enough for your puppy to stand up and turn around in comfortably.

*Consider whether you want a puppy playpen or gates/barriers to help keep your puppy contained in a small area (he is going to be into everything).

*For yourself I suggest having a supply of disposable gloves, and some hand-cream (because your hands are going to get scratched and bitten by your new furry friend, not to mention dry because of all that extra hand washing you're going to be doing).

And therein ends the list. Phew! You can get more things as you go along.

If you aren't sure which breed to go for, do lots of research. Do you want a large dog or a smaller one? Does slobbering bother you? How much of your time do you mind devoting to cleaning up dog hair? Do you love going for long walks on a daily basis? Basically, choose a dog which suits both your lifestyle and your accommodation. If you live in a flat for example, in order to keep your neighbours happy you'll want a breed which doesn't bark too much. And is the breed suited to living in a flat?

Archie is a cross between a Bichon Frise and a Shih Tzu, which means double helpings of mischief. Zuchons are also called Shichon and Teddy Bear dogs.

One of the reasons we decided we wanted a Zuchon was because of how cute they are – superficial, I know – but there were practical reasons too, such as the size they tend to grow to (we wanted a small dog), and the fact Zuchons are low shedding dogs.

Zuchons have two layers of hair, which is very high maintenance. Although they don't shed much their hair matts easily and so daily brushing is required in order to keep it matt free. On the plus side, Zuchons are hypoallergenic, which means if you thought you couldn't have a dog due to having allergies, you might be okay with a Zuchon (please note a reaction could still occur).

Zuchons are very sociable. They don't like being on their own and will follow you around. Archie is so affectionate. He's always up for some fun; he's curious too. He's good with other dogs. He doesn't need a lot of exercise; a couple of short walks per day and some playtime, together with some training and puzzle games, makes for a happy dog.

I will say this breed has a tendency to be hyperactive – some are more chilled out than others. And they can be stubborn. Trainers may disagree with me here, but other Zuchon owners will know what I mean!

Do get some advice on choosing a puppy and what questions to ask the breeder (including microchipping which is a legal requirement in the UK). I found some useful information on the Dogs Trust website. And savour the moment – I'll never forget seeing Archie for the first time. He was so tiny he fitted in Simon's hand.

Before you bring your puppy home, try to puppy-proof your house as much as possible. Think outside the box – I didn't think I needed to put my CD rack away, for example, but a certain furry friend liked chewing the plastic cases.

Archie loves helping himself to a tissue from the wastepaper bin, and initially we put all the bins out of his reach, or emptied them more often. He still likes doing it, so now we've cut down on the amount of wastepaper bins we have, and the bins we have got are all the pedestal kind.

If you do leave things out you'll have to be prepared not to leave your puppy unsupervised. An alternative would be to pop him in a puppy playpen or a crate (if you can withstand the crying), so your pup is safely contained whilst you're busy.

'I wish I'd relaxed more with Archie when he was a young pup. I was too anxious though.'

POST PUPPY BLUES

Simon and I haven't got kids, but one of Simon's work colleagues told him they'd found bringing up a puppy harder than bringing up a baby! It just goes to show that a tiny puppy can have a massive impact on your life. You're suddenly responsible for this little creature who is entirely dependent upon you.

I worried whether we were doing things the right way, whether Archie was happy with us. I felt like I couldn't cope. To outsiders everything looked rosy. Here was this gorgeous little puppy, who charmed everyone he met. Why was I feeling so negative? Had we made a huge mistake?

Quite simply, I had a bad case of what we'll call 'the puppy blues'. Here was a tiny scrap of a thing that I was 100% responsible for. I'd never been responsible for anyone before. I worked part-time, whilst my husband worked full-time, so I spent more time with Archie. I used to dread the days when I wasn't working – a whole eight hours or more on my own with Archie. He didn't seem to sleep all that much and needed to be watched constantly.

I felt like my life had narrowed because I wasn't able to do simple things like read a book, or write (I'm also a freelance writer) whenever I wanted to as I'd been used to doing before Archie came along. I couldn't leave him for long, and he couldn't be taken for a walk until he'd had his second vaccination. I couldn't take him in a shop with me (unless it was Pets at Home). I was nervous about driving with him in the back of the car. And constantly cleaning up after Archie left me feeling drab and dirty.

I'm an anxious person anyway, and getting a puppy made me even more anxious than usual. In all the excitement, I didn't anticipate this. It would have helped if I had – I don't think I would have been so hard on myself. I felt like I was a terrible person for not being able to enjoy Archie during those early days, and for having thoughts of giving him up.

I didn't feel like I could talk to anyone else apart from Simon about it, but of course, he was going through it too (although not as bad). Thankfully we each had our down moments at different times, so were able to comfort each other. When I tried to talk about it to other people, I quickly learnt to change the subject or make a joke of it, because they just didn't understand. They only wanted to hear about the nice things.

Then, searching online, I found other people who'd had the same feelings, who'd gone through the exact same thing. It was comforting to know I wasn't alone, and it made me feel better to read other people's stories.

All the advice said to get through the first few months and that things would improve. As time passed I found I was coping. I remember having a meltdown over Archie's dirty bottom on the first day I was left on my own with him. Now I don't think anything of it; I just scoop him up and put him in the shower – job done.

There's a flip side, too. Archie has helped me with the intermittent anxiety I have felt over my job. If I've been worried about a meeting, for example, spending time with him has made me realise the importance of living in the present, of prioritising. If I'm having a stressful day it helps to think about playing with Archie when I get home from work. Cuddles help too!

'It always makes me smile the way Archie runs to the kitchen when he hears me putting his bowl of food on the floor.'

ALL ABOUT FOOD

You shouldn't switch your dog's food suddenly in case he gets sick, but we didn't have much choice. Although the breeder gave us some of the food she'd been giving Archie and his siblings, during Archie's early days with us he had diarrhoea, so I had to resort to plain food like chicken, rice, and scrambled egg. Once he'd recovered, he didn't want his normal food. As I wasn't overly keen on the ingredients in the brand of food the breeder gave us, I decided to make the switch, and researched other wet dog food. I eventually decided on some puppy food which was aimed at sensitive tummies.

Archie took to the new food quickly and his poos were firm – always a good sign. I wanted Archie to eat a mixture of wet and dry dog food (I find kibble is more cost effective) and so I bought some kibble, also for sensitive tummies, and introduced it slowly. Again, no problems.

Once Archie had been neutered (aged around nine months) I noticed he was eating less. Frequently he'd skip breakfast, but thankfully he almost always ate his tea. I know the standard advice is not to worry, not to give in and offer meat instead of the usual food, that after skipping a meal or two your puppy will be hungry and want to eat whatever's put before him. It's hard though, when your pet's not eating.

It never got so bad that Archie wasn't eating at all; if he'd shown any signs of being poorly, I would have taken him to see a vet, but he was a happy, lively puppy. I experimented with his food; I tried a different brand of wet food – getting the adult version because the instructions indicated this was appropriate for Archie's age and weight. I introduced it slowly, a little at a time with his regular food, and his appetite returned.

Archie later went through a phase of not wanting to eat wet food – just kibble – and then he went through a phase of only eating wet food. Nowadays he's back to eating a mixture of the two, and I have changed brands again. He runs to his bowl at mealtimes. I sometimes warm the kibble in the microwave, to make it that bit more tasty for him. His coat is glossy, his teeth are in excellent condition, I've noticed the tear-staining isn't so bad (more on this later), and he is a cheeky boy. The food obviously suits him.

I do sometimes give Archie "human" food, like chicken or some scrambled egg. I add it to his kibble, although too big a portion – of chicken, for example – can affect the consistency of his poos, so I limit it to a spoonful (please note some dogs can be allergic / intolerant to chicken. Just like humans, dogs can have allergies too).

If Archie has treats for training purposes, or any extras like the aforementioned chicken, I reduce his main food accordingly; I don't want him to become overweight.

You will see that I have been careful not to name any brand names here, food-wise. That is because for all the positive reviews you find of a particular dog food, there will inevitably be negative reviews. What suits one dog won't suit another. Do your research. Look at the ingredients – the percentage of meat and also what cut of meat it is. Is it a by-product or meal, which aren't the best quality and which aren't given to humans, so would you want your dog eating it? Look for fillers etc. Be discerning. You know your dog best. If his food doesn't seem to be suiting him, or he doesn't seem to like it, slowly introduce a different type. Experiment with wet and dry food. Eventually you'll find one that suits.

Let the person looking after your dog know your stance on food treats, especially if they're likely to feed your dog human food (I'm thinking about Archie's two grannies here, who do love to slip him a bit of sausage or chicken, biscuits or even cake!)

Look up which human foods can be dangerous for your dog (plus plants, flowers, garden and household substances). Again the Dogs Trust website has some useful information.

'Prepare yourself for numerous conversations about poo.'

HEALTHY PUPPY

Insurance
It stands to reason that your dog is going to need treatment at some stage, and insurance is going to help with the bills. Not all policies are the same. Read what is and isn't covered and compare policies. I would definitely recommend getting lifetime cover because it offers the most protection, although there will still be limits.

The sooner you take out pet insurance the better because you can't make any claims for accidents which occur during the first few days of the policy, nor can you make a claim for any illnesses which show symptoms during the early days of the policy.

Vet
Get your puppy registered with a vet as soon as you can because you never know when you'll need to go.

It's a good idea to go to the veterinary centre regularly when your puppy's young, and to make it a positive experience, so that future visits will be a breeze. Go to puppy parties, take your puppy to be wormed – even to have his nails clipped. The staff always make a big fuss of him, so for Archie, it's always been a treat to go to the vet's.

Flea treatment
Archie has never had fleas – I hope he never has them – and he takes a tablet every 12 weeks as a preventative measure. Speak to your vet about this.

Neuter
Although we felt guilty about getting Archie castrated, we felt it was for the best, since we didn't want him fathering any puppies. Our vet told us that neutering also helps to reduce the chances of male dogs getting prostate disease.

There were no complications with the procedure and we went to pick Archie up mid-afternoon the same day. He was a little groggy, but his tail was still wagging.

When we got him home he ate his tea and then he slept pretty much until the following morning, at which point he was a little livelier. He ate his breakfast, but had diarrhoea later. We took him for a short walk and he wasn't bothering his wound too much.

The following day he was back to his usual cheeky self. The nurse had told us to try to keep him quiet – no running around and not to let him jump on the furniture. It's very difficult to slow down an active puppy! Thankfully Archie's wound continued to heal nicely.

When we took him back to the veterinary centre for a post-op check they were happy with him. The diarrhoea had stopped, thank goodness. We mentioned it to the nurse and she said it was normal after surgery.

A couple of weeks after the surgery, however, a red lump appeared on his wound and so we took Archie back to the vet's to get it checked out. They said it was nothing to worry about – one of the sutures had popped out. Because Archie had started licking it we bought an inflatable collar for him to wear during the day. We wanted to avoid the cone-type, and the inflatable version was soft and Archie didn't seem bothered by it at all. I didn't want him to have to sleep in it, though, so I bought a cheap pair of boys' shorts from the supermarket – he looked so funny!

Thankfully just a couple of weeks later his wound had healed completely.

Poo

I have never talked about poo – dog poo, I hasten to add – as much as I did during the first year we had Archie. The colour, the consistency, the frequency … For a long time the first words my husband and I exchanged each morning were whether or not Archie had done a poo. In fact, I thought about calling this book, '*Two Wees and a Poo*' (Archie's toileting routine first thing every morning), but it's not the most inviting title.

I never thought I'd be grateful for normal poo, but I was when Archie had diarrhoea in the early days and appeared to be producing Korma sauce (note: cleaning up sloppy poo from the pavement isn't easy!) We had to take him to the vet's where he had his bum examined and was given a special paste to take. It was like a miracle cure – his poos quickly firmed up.

My advice – invest in some machine washable rugs – they're easier to keep clean. And we decided to invest in a carpet cleaner, or if you don't want to do that, you could hire one from time to time.

A quick note on the subject of flooring; there's a danger your puppy may slip on wooden or laminate flooring so rugs and runners (with a non-slip mat underneath them), would be a good idea anyway.

Worming
Puppies need worming regularly, and we used to take Archie to the vet's to be wormed. The nurse clinics are free, and you can get your puppy weighed whilst you're there. I've decided to keep worming Archie as a preventative measure. Now that he's big enough/old enough for us to give him the tablets at home, we buy them direct from the veterinary centre – I hide the tablets in his food.

'Puppies seem delighted to get themselves dirty, like when Archie rubs his head in fox poo, or when he tries to dig his way to Australia in our back garden.'

MUCKY PUPPY

Archie has the type of hair which matts easily. When he was a young pup I bought a soft bristle brush for him, but it turned out to be ineffective in terms of keeping the matting at bay. I was really concerned about this, since the dog trainer we saw warned us that it's very painful for dogs if their hair matts and needs to be shaved off.

When I took Archie for his first proper groom he had a few matts, which I'd tried to get out, only I learned I didn't have the right brush. The groomer didn't seem too concerned. She had all the right tools and she got the matts out, gave Archie a wash and a trim and he came out smelling gorgeous (I wish he smelt like that all the time!). He licked the groomer so much that it was obvious he hadn't been traumatised by the experience.

The groomer recommended a slicker brush, and it was great in the early days. A quick going over left Archie all fluffy, but as the texture of his hair changed as he grew older, I found it wasn't up to the task of dealing with the matting.

Next I bought a comb from Pets at Home. It did the job, but it was time-consuming using it all over his body. Then a friend recommended a de-matter, which looks more than a little scary. It was great for getting matts out, but Archie didn't like it. These days I use a double-sided comb, which for under £5 has been one of my best purchases. Archie has to have a full groom fairly often, every six to eight weeks, because keeping his hair matt free when it's longer is too time consuming.

Drying Archie used to be difficult because he hated the hair dryer. We used to have to feed him treats whilst we dried him (I held the hair dryer whilst Simon brushed Archie), but it stopped working. Then I tried putting some peanut butter on one of his chews for him to lick, which did the trick. Kong paste also worked. We've made a lot of progress as nowadays, when Archie's finished licking the peanut butter, he just stands there and lets me finish drying him. He's as good as gold as long as I don't go near his face – I let the hair round his face and neck dry naturally.

I also bought Archie a drying robe. It's the doggy version of a dressing gown, which helps to dry your dog's hair more quickly. As it only takes around twenty minutes for Archie's hair to dry whilst wearing the robe (no hairdryer required), I think it was a good investment.

Washing Archie isn't so bad. When he was really small we used to put him in a washing up bowl. He cried a bit. Now he's bigger we use the shower – it's so much quicker – and he no longer cries, although he still doesn't like his head getting wet, and so I use a wet flannel round his beard and so on. I used to use puppy shampoo, but now Archie's older I use shampoo specifically for white hair, which makes it shine and smell of blueberries.

If your puppy has rubbed himself in fox poo, you might need to shampoo him more than once in order to get rid of the smell (it stinks!) You can buy shampoo specifically for fox poo.

Come autumn, Archie gets filthy during a walk. He's mostly white, and his tummy and legs get splattered with dirty water, so he needs a rinse in the shower.

We clean Archie's paws daily – even during the summer. It's more hygienic, because not every dog owner picks up their dog's poo and sometimes Archie steps in it. Taking a few minutes to rinse Archie's paws means less dirt in the house. If it's wet outside we also wipe Archie's paws when he comes in from the garden. We've done this since the early days so he's used to it.

We don't have snow very often, but last winter we had a lot of the white stuff, and it stayed around for a few days. Archie's legs got covered in mini snow balls every time we went out for a walk! To get snow balls off your dog quickly, put him in the shower and rinse the affected areas in lukewarm water.

Archie hates having under his eyes cleaned, but the gunk builds up, so I have to persevere. And he had tear stains – that reddish tinge you see sometimes under their eyes. I use some cotton wool pads dipped in warm water, and give Archie treats whilst I'm doing it, this way he tolerates it for the most part. The tear-staining isn't so prominent now. I did check with the vet about it, because it can sometimes indicate an eye health problem, but in Archie's case it's inherent to the breed. Diet can also be a factor.

Nor does Archie like having his ears cleaned. He won't tolerate ear drops, but I've got some special ear wipes and over time he's got used to them. He used to hate having his ears touched at all, but he's much better now. Treats help!

I bought some tooth gel, which just needed to be rubbed along Archie's gums. The idea is that as your dog licks it off his gums, he spreads it over his teeth. Archie likes it, although he does keep trying to lick it off my finger before I've managed to rub it on his gums.

I noticed some plaque building up on his teeth though, and realised the tooth gel wasn't enough, and so I started getting Archie used to having his teeth brushed. I bought a toothbrush and toothpaste from Pets at Home, and he's taken to it quite well. I think it helped that he was already used to me putting gel on his gums. I still use the gel at times, and I have also found some dental chews Archie likes – the plaque has gone!

'I rarely leave Pets at Home without a new toy for Archie.'

PLAY-TIME

Buy different types of toys for your puppy and find out what he likes. Lots of dogs like playing tug – Archie, not so much. He adores playing hide and seek and it's fun for us too. This game is a quick and easy way to keep your pup entertained. Best played with two people, all you need is some treats. Take it in turns to call your puppy, moving into a different room each time, and have him come and find you. This combines play with training as each time you'll be asking your pup to 'come here'. And in time you can add on other commands.

Archie loves playing fetch, but although he'll run for the ball, he doesn't always return with it. I don't think it's a lack of understanding on his part. The little monkey thinks it's great fun for one of us to go and get the ball. We've begun teaching Archie the 'bring it' command, so that he will bring the ball to us, and we're having more success with this.

Physical exercise is important, but your dog also needs mental stimulation. This will tire him out in a different way, and he won't have time to be bored and go chew your slippers! Try different puzzle toys or teach him the 'go find' command so you can hide treats or toys and have him sniff them out.

A treat ball was a success with Archie when he was younger, Kongs, less so. Every pup is different.

Puppies and young dogs will have periods when they run round like they're possessed. This is nothing to worry about – they are just using up some excess energy. They will tire themselves out very quickly.

'No matter how nice your puppy's basket is, they will always prefer to be on your bed!'

Basket

I wish now that initially we hadn't bought Archie such a big basket. We bought a medium-sized one, thinking he'd grow into it and we wouldn't need to buy another one for a while. In the early days he was swamped by it. He's much happier in his faux fur basket (light grey), which I bought when he'd grown a bit. He definitely likes soft furry materials, and is attracted to lighter colours. He curls up in this one during the day, which he rarely did in his old one. My advice is not to spend much money on a basket until you've discovered what your puppy likes.

Bed

When we first got Archie we decided we wouldn't allow him on our bed, but when he was big enough to jump up by himself, we realised he liked to lie on it and look out of the window and people (and dog) watch. At the time our bedroom faced the road you see. So when Archie was toilet-trained and we knew we could trust him, we allowed him on the bed during the day. It was a gradual process.

For a long time we stuck to not letting him sleep in the bedroom at night. We doubted he would stay in his basket in the corner of the room, and we didn't want him on the bed with us because he moves around so much! So Archie slept in the hall – as we live in a bungalow he wasn't far away.

Then we went on holiday and inevitably Archie ended up sleeping in our bedroom with us. He'd start off the night in his basket, but at some point during the early hours of the morning he'd join us on the bed. If we put him back in his basket, he'd soon return, and in the end we gave up. We got used to him nestling in-between us.

When we returned home Archie made a fuss about being left in the hall at night. I suppose we could have persevered and got him used to sleeping in the hall again, but we didn't mind him sleeping in the bedroom so long as he was in his basket for some of the time. And that's our current routine.

Blankets

You can never have enough blankets and throws where dogs are concerned, throws (though watch for any sign of them being chewed). Throws to protect the sofa, of course, and possibly the bed if you don't mind your dog going on it. Blankets for your puppy to snuggle up on. That said, Archie will also have a snooze on the laminate floor. Something to bear in mind – you might neatly arrange a blanket in your pup's basket, yet he will quickly mess it up. Archie rearranges a blanket until it's to his liking! It's funny to watch.

Crate

When Archie was very small, we bought a fabric crate. He wouldn't use it in the house (we did get some use from it in the car). When we put him in it he cried, despite us trying to get him used to it slowly. And I know you're supposed to ignore the crying, but he went on and on … If you've never heard a puppy cry, well, it's very difficult to ignore.

We bought a metal crate for Archie when he was more or less fully grown. We got one big enough for him to stand up and turn around in comfortably. I never liked the idea of a crate in the beginning – it's basically a cage – but I know some people swear by them for toilet training. I changed my mind because I thought Archie needed his own den.

The fabric crate we used to have, despite having a mesh window, didn't give Archie a great view. The metal crate we've got now, and which we've put in the lounge, allows him to see round the room. It's lined with vet bedding, and again, we took the time to get him used to it, putting treats or his favourite chews inside and praising him whenever he went in there. He did this quite happily, but only stayed long enough to eat his treats. We occasionally put him in there if he wouldn't settle down during the evening and we wanted to watch TV, and that's the only time we closed the door. He settled, and I think he got the message, because we have no need to do that now.

When we moved house, I had to try the crate in different positions for Archie before we found the right spot, and Archie now goes in it to sleep sometimes during the day. I put a blanket over the top, which I think has helped make it cosier for him.

It's a good idea to get your puppy familiar with a crate even if you're not using it for toilet training, because it will be less upsetting for him if he has to stay at the vet's in the future as they routinely use crates. Similarly, if dogs ever have to have an operation, and need to be kept quiet when they're back home in order to convalesce, then a crate is going to be essential.

Archie has created another den himself. He loves the gap between the footstool and the sofa. Dogs are funny!

'Archie gets so excited when he goes to doggy daycare – I don't get a look-in when I drop him off!'

SOCIALISATION MATTERS

Your puppy needs to meet lots of people and other dogs, and have lots of experiences – the aim is a well-adjusted adult dog. Here are a few suggestions:

Doggy Daycare

I took Archie to a petsitter in our village a few times, but she had another job and couldn't always look after Archie when I needed her to, so I decided to look for another petsitter. This led me to the DogBuddy website. I entered my postcode and found some petsitters who lived nearby. There was one in particular I liked the look of. She had a dog of her own, and her love of animals – dogs in particular – shone through.

We took Archie to meet Paula one evening. Her partner was there, along with her dog, Tilly, and a few other dogs who were staying overnight. Paula was lovely with Archie (as was her partner), and Archie seemed to get on with Tilly, too. We had a good chat and arranged for Archie to spend a day there later that same week.

On Archie's first day with Paula she told me that initially she would keep Archie separate from the other dogs, so that he wasn't overwhelmed. He would spend some time with Tilly, and meet the other dogs gradually. A group walk was also planned for later in the day.

I received text updates and photos during the day, which reassured me. Archie looked like he was having a ball. When I went to pick him up he greeted me enthusiastically, but he also ran back to Paula, which I took to be a good sign.

I think the DogBuddy site is brilliant because you can read reviews, see pictures, bookings are covered by public liability and vet insurance, and there's a 24/7 emergency vet line. You pay via the site and receive confirmation of the booking.

Archie was going to Paula's for one day a week before we relocated. It felt good to be able to go to work knowing he was having fun (more fun than I was having that's for sure). I can't recommend doggy daycare highly enough. It helps your dog to get used to being around other dogs. And Archie got used to Paula's home so that when I booked him in for a week (when my husband and I went on holiday), he was comfortable there.

I found it incredibly hard to leave Archie behind when I went on holiday, and I don't think I'll be doing it very often. I felt so guilty leaving him, despite knowing he'd be well looked after. I missed him too. Paula sent me daily updates, and I could see he was having a great time, which helped a lot.

Pets at Home

Pets at Home is a great place to take your pooch – stock up on supplies and socialise your pup at the same time. Be warned – it can take a while to get round the store since everyone (staff and fellow customers alike) will want to meet your furry friend.

Puppy Hour

We discovered a puppy hour was being held every Saturday morning at our local Wyevale Garden Centre (in Pets Corner), and so we took Archie there several times. There were pups of all different sizes, some running around like crazy things, whilst others were more timid. There's a discount for any purchases made during puppy hour.

Puppy Parties

The veterinary centre we used to take Archie to ran regular puppy parties, and Archie received an invite to one when we registered him there. The party ran for around two hours. There were ten puppies there, all of a similar size. Archie made friends with a female puppy, who followed him everywhere.

The veterinary nurses left out lots of toys for the puppies to play with. We were also given some health tips. It was very useful (and free), so it's worth checking out whether your veterinary centre holds puppy parties.

Take your puppy everywhere you can – taking him to new places will also provide him with mental stimulation. Take him outside when the recycling is being collected. Take him to your friend's house. Involve him in your life. And carry on doing it, even as your dog gets older. He'll always be interested in new sights, sounds and, of course, smells.

'I'm wondering whether I'll ever have a decent sofa again.'

TRAINING YOUR PUPPY

Commands

Archie had 1:1 training sessions at home. In the early days we were panicking – not sure we were doing the right things – and so we wanted some advice. Evelyn, our dog trainer (who I found via Google), was wonderful. She came to our house, looked at Archie's toileting routine and gave us some tips. She also started him/us off with the main commands: **Sit, Stand, Down** (as in lie-down), **Follow Me** etc. And whenever Archie took a nap, as puppies are wont to do, she answered any general queries we had about bringing up a puppy. She gave us a confidence boost, and it meant Archie learnt the main commands early on.

Because Archie knew all the commands, we only took him to a class for socialisation purposes, but as there was only one other puppy in the class it wasn't ideal. We didn't finish the course and instead started booking Archie into doggie day care so he could meet other dogs. I know a lot of people swear by classes, and if Archie hadn't had private training sessions, we would have carried on with the course, although we would have switched to a larger class. If you're looking for a class ask other dog owners or search online. I noticed that my local Pets at Home store runs puppy classes, so it's worth checking your local store, and the veterinary centre you go to may have details of classes too.

Once your puppy has mastered the commands inside your home, try doing them outside with him. There will be more distractions, which is why it's important to train your dog to follow commands outside, too. Go back to basics, take the treats with you, and get your dog to sit on the pavement, wait at the kerb etc.

I'm not going to go over the main commands, because you'll learn them in puppy class or via one of the numerous books on the subject, but below I've shared some of the commands which I've found particularly helpful:

Wait – We first started teaching this command to Archie at mealtimes. We'd put his bowl down, and get him to wait. He learnt quickly.

No – Teach your dog what this word means. It's a very useful command. Simply have a treat in your hand, but when your dog goes to take it, curl your hand into a fist and say 'no'.

Leave It – We taught this command to Archie very early on. The neighbourhood cats liked to do their business in our back garden, and we often found a new deposit there. Archie naturally wanted to know what it was! We'd pull him away from it, saying 'leave it' as we did so.

Settle – This is another good command to teach your dog. You simply have to say it when they've settled down of their own accord. Say something like, 'Good, settle, good boy.' Also praise him for doing nothing, for quiet behaviour.

In general, praise the behaviour you do want, whilst ignoring the behaviour you don't want (that's if it's safe to do so. Obviously move him away from the cable he's happily started to chew!)

We never shout at Archie, but I do sometimes say 'uh oh' if he doesn't do as I ask, or I'll say 'no' very firmly if he's chewing something he shouldn't.

Biting
The best advice regarding Archie trying to bite us when he was very small, came from our trainer; she told us to yelp loudly, and if he carried on, to stop all play immediately and to turn our backs on him. Puppies soon learn that if they don't play nice, the play stops. They do grow out of it –

Archie did - so don't despair if you don't think it's working. At the time, I remember thinking I had a mini-crocodile, so I do sympathise. And when the biting has been reduced to mouthing, you can teach your puppy not to do that either.

Chewing

Puppies chew, there's nothing new about that. Since I remembered the puppy we had when I was a child liked to chew the telephone cable, we hid our cables as best we could – and I thought we were prepared for Archie. And yes, he liked trying to get hold of cables, and footwear was also fair game, but we didn't bargain on him chewing books, CDs, the wastepaper bins (wicker was a real draw), my Kindle, our phones, the vertical blind slats …

Puppies will try to eat almost anything. We tried spraying things like our slippers and the bottom of the sofa with some special deterrent spray (from Pets at Home), but it didn't stop Archie. I've lost count of how many pairs of slippers we've gone through, and I learnt to buy very plain slippers. If they were fluffy or had something like a bow on them, it made them even more attractive to Archie.

Give your puppy something legitimate to chew (it should be durable, but not too hard for their teeth). We've bought Archie a variety of chew toys. It's trial and error finding out what your puppy likes. Successes with Archie have included rope toys, various Nylabone chews, and a spiky treat ball.

Giving your puppy some frozen vegetables like peas and carrots to eat may help with the teething process, or maybe some crushed ice. There are also chew toys you can freeze, and toys you can fill with water and freeze (which can also help your dog to keep cool during the summer).

Archie doesn't try to chew everything in sight now, and he will respond to 'no' and 'leave it', but he still has his moments when we're not in the room and we've forgotten to put something away. It's easy to forget, which means some of my things, including my Kindle cover and a pair of boots, have little teeth marks on them. And he's got hold of my glasses more than once – my fault for leaving them out. Footwear is still a firm favourite. Apart from things on the floor, think about things you've left on the arm of the sofa, even on a side table which your puppy can reach from the sofa.

Ah yes, the sofa. You might want to hide your best cushions, and only put out some cheap ones, or at the very least, have cushions with washable covers. I often walk into the lounge and find cushions on the floor. I can't blame Archie for thinking they're toys – they must feel like a soft toy in his mouth. He used to like to "dig" on the sofa, but he's stopped doing that; he rolls around on it instead!

Beware silence. Sometimes it can indeed mean your puppy is asleep. At other times it means your puppy is gleefully chewing on something he shouldn't, and which he could potentially choke on, or have a poorly tummy (or worse) if he manages to eat it.

Desensitisation

I read about a sound effects CD, which can help to desensitise puppies to various noises – fireworks being a good example. I didn't buy a CD because I found an app via the Google Play store (Sound Proof Puppy Training), which cost £2.69 at the time, and I gradually exposed Archie to the sounds of fireworks, amongst other things. When November came round, Archie didn't seem fazed by fireworks.

There are lots of other sound effects on the app including clippers, motorbikes, thunder, drills, lawn mowers, and vacuum cleaners.

Before we moved, we took Archie to see our new home a couple of times before we moved in. For moving day we also bought an Adaptil diffuser, which can help to calm dogs during times of stress. Archie settled in quickly. I can't say for sure whether the Adaptil plug-in helped or not, but I'm glad we got it, regardless.

Me-Time

Dogs can be manipulative. One morning Archie was whining to be let in the bedroom. I was having a lie-in, and I didn't want to let him in because he was still wet from being out in the garden. He wasn't on his own, my husband was around, but Archie's a bed hog – hence the whining. I didn't give in. I made him wait, and a bit later on I let him in the room, but only because he was quiet. I don't want him thinking he'll get his own way every time he whines. Sure enough, the second he was let in the bedroom, he was happy, tail wagging etc.

Dogs want to be with you all the time, but they have to learn they can't have your attention 24/7. Don't give in too much, otherwise you'll be setting a pattern and you'll never get any peace. I'll be sat at my desk in my home office and Archie will try to get on my lap. It's difficult to type with a dog on your lap, and so I give him a cuddle and then put him in his basket by the side of me. It mostly works!

Quiet Times

I have tried to teach Archie to calm down. He comes home after doggy daycare and he still wants to play, when in theory he should be tired. I've realised it's because he's overstimulated. I simply get hold of him, put him on my lap, and stroke him, saying 'calm' occasionally to him. It works – he's soon nodding off.

Toilet Training

Aah, I remember it well. It's not pleasant, but as your puppy grows, so too will his bladder, and before long he'll be able to hold his wee overnight.

There are going to be numerous accidents around the house, so it's best to limit where your puppy goes in the early days. Take him outside often, and praise him whenever he does his business in the garden (have a treat ready for him too). If he does something indoors, don't shout for he may start to become afraid of you and do things behind your back.

You don't want him doing his business behind the sofa! Just scoop him up and take him outdoors, then calmly clean the mess up when you go back indoors. This is all assuming you're not using a crate to toilet train your puppy – we didn't.

Sometimes, if you can tell your puppy's just about to squat, you can pick him up and taken him outside. It will be like Ground Hog day, until eventually you're going outside less and less. He'll get it. And in the meantime you need to recognise the signs when he want to go out, e.g. he'll be pacing and won't be able to settle.

I also started to say 'wee' whilst Archie was doing one, so now, if we're due to go somewhere in the car, I can say 'wee' to him and he'll do one pretty much on demand.

Whilst your puppy is toilet training, unless you're prepared to get up in the night to take him out, you'll have to put newspaper or puppy pads down in the area he's sleeping in. That's what we did. Spread them everywhere, because initially your puppy will do his business in random places (although always away from his bed). He will eventually start using one spot, until one day you get up and there is no mess whatsoever to clean up. Happy days.

We tried various brands of puppy pads whilst Archie was being toilet-trained. The quality varied. I thought the best ones at the time (as well as being excellent value for money) were by the RSPCA.

I bought a puppy pad holder because li'l Archie had a habit of picking up the pads when they were loose and running round the lounge with them. Next he tried to eat them! He was still able to chew the edges of the pad when it was in the pad holder, so it didn't help.

We bought some special pet barriers to stop Archie going in certain parts of the house when he wasn't toilet-trained. One type, which we bought from Argos, didn't need to be fixed to the wall. The other type, which we bought from B&Q, did need fixing to the wall and was very similar to a baby gate, with a door which opens. Archie wasn't big enough to jump over either of them, and they were very useful.

Just when you think things are calming down and you're over the worst, comes the teenage phase. It's not pleasant. Archie stopped listening to us; the chewing intensified; he was constantly nipping at us, and he was hyperactive. Nothing seemed to work. You just have to grit your teeth, be consistent, keep to a routine, keep training, maybe increase the length of the walk and so on. It's just a phase and it will pass.

'One programme I watched said that a lamppost is the doggy form of Twitter. It makes me smile now whenever I see Archie sniffing a lamppost.'

WALKIES

Getting to know what your dog needs/likes walk-wise takes time. Walks were getting so frustrating as Archie kept sitting down and seemed reluctant to walk. I didn't want to keep pulling him along. I felt he needed to be able to walk at his own pace, and to stop and sniff and basically have more freedom. Of course, that's all well and good if your dog has a reliable recall – you could let him off his lead – but we're not at that stage with Archie yet.

We'd love to let Archie off his lead more. We tried it a few times in the fields, but he didn't always come back straightaway when we called him (despite the lure of treats), so there was obviously more work to do regarding the 'come here' command.

We bought an extending lead for Archie and it made a huge difference. It means he can have more freedom during a walk, but he can still be safely reigned in if needs be. He trots around happily and you'd swear he was smiling. I've also realised that 30mins is his limit for one walk, and then he gets tired. Nowadays he has two walks a day, one in the morning and one early afternoon.

When we moved house and gained a large (enclosed) back garden, we were able to do a lot more recall practise. Archie now nearly always comes when we call, but not when he's distracted, and so I still don't feel confident enough to allow him to walk off-leash.

I'm not going to worry about it. I was watching an episode of *Supervet* recently, and the story of how a dog who ran after a fox got knocked over made me think. I don't want to lose my dog, or for him to be hurt and need complex surgery, and so keeping him on the lead is the safest option. Archie gets to run freely round his own garden, so he's not missing out.

We are still working on Archie's recall. I wondered if using a whistle might help. I bought an Acme 210.5 whistle from Amazon. I am slowly trying to get Archie to associate the sound of the whistle with positive things – treats – and eventually hope to train him to come back to me whenever he hears it. The whistle means we have a fresh start with recall training. The down side is I will always need to have it with me when we're out.

Know that you're committing to take your puppy out for a walk at least once a day. Get kitted out for inclement weather – you and your puppy – and be prepared to wash him when you get home or at least give him a towel rub. It can get boring, taking the same route every day, so try to vary it. And it's better if you're with someone else, so you can chat whilst your dog sniffs.

For walks, we've always used a harness, so Archie's used to wearing one now. I don't like the idea of using a collar and lead, because I'm concerned about hurting his neck if I have to pull him away from another dog's poo. I don't want him eating poo for hygiene reasons, but we were also told at the vet's that the most common way in which the potentially fatal parvo virus is spread is when a dog comes into contact with an infected dog's poo.

If you're likely to be walking your dog in the dark, then buy reflective gear for both you and your dog. I have a torch I take too, whilst my husband bought a head torch. I also bought a small flashing keyring light which clips onto Archie's harness.

'Always take more poo bags with you than you think you'll need.'

Leaving the house with your pup for a walk or a car journey means you'll need to allow a bit more time to get ready than you normally would.

If you're going on a walk you'll need poo bags for starters; some water depending upon how warm it is/how long the walk will be; some treats for training opportunities outside. You may or may not need to chase your puppy in order to get his harness on – this is a game Archie plays.

For the car it will depend where you're going, what you're doing, how long you're going to be out for, as to what you'll need to take with you. Be prepared to stop for toilet breaks and a stretch of the legs. I keep an old towel in the car too, either to clean Archie's paws or dry him off if it's been raining.

The same goes for if you're leaving the house for a little while and you're leaving your puppy behind. You'll need to make sure your puppy has some company and stimulation – a walk or a play – before you leave, that he's eaten (ideally), that he has access to some treats, toys, water etc. Make sure the doors to the rooms you don't want him to go in are closed, and that there's nothing lying around that he could chew. This is all assuming you're not using a crate.

Car

It is now law in the UK that dogs must be suitably restrained when in the car. Archie has his own seatbelt in both mine and my husband's cars. One end clips into the seatbelt holder, whilst the other clips onto Archie's harness. In the early days we put Archie in a fabric crate in the car, but he outgrew it, and as he couldn't see much in it, we decided not to replace it with a bigger crate. Instead, we bought a waterproof seat cover. We put a blanket on top of that and Archie either sits or lies down on it, depending upon how tired he is. He likes to sit up and see what's going on and it means he gets more stimulation. The seatbelt has been great, and was surprisingly inexpensive. I found it on Amazon.

Archie used to bark a lot in the car. I think he was over-excited. We dreaded longer journeys and took earplugs to wear. Thankfully, he doesn't bark so much now in the car, and only does it when we stop and get out. Again, he's excited.

Don't let your dog get too energetic straight after eating, or take him out in the car. Leave at least half-an-hour, if not a full hour, otherwise he might be sick.

'I now understand people who are dotty about their dog, because I'm one of them.'

Two years on and I'm so much more confident and relaxed, and best of all, I've got a happy, healthy, gorgeous dog. Thank goodness those early days are behind us. I've always thought that as well as us getting to know Archie, Archie had to get to know – and put up with – Simon and me learning as we went along.

I often think about a guy we met in Pets at Home. We hadn't had Archie for long and we were feeling shell-shocked. This guy stopped to talk to us and made a fuss of Archie. He was further along the path than us – he'd been a puppy parent for longer. He said he'd found it a nightmare initially, but that it got easier as time went on, and now he wouldn't be without his dog. He will never know how much he helped us. We left the store feeling cheered and encouraged. And that's precisely what I'm trying to do with this book – help and encourage new puppy parents.

If you're feeling anxious about your puppy, then I'm sending you a virtual hug. Everything is going to be alright – it really is. If you're finding it tough, take it a day at a time and things will improve. You'll get to know your puppy, you'll bond, and remember, the toilet training can only get better!

There is a lot of advice on the internet, some of it helpful, some of it not, a lot of it contradictory. Read widely, see what resonates, try some of it out, but most of all go with your instincts.

I have found being a member of a group of Zuchon owners on Facebook to be very helpful, so look for something similar. It's great to get tips, read other people's stories, and to see all the lovely dogs out there.

Life will never be the same again, and I'm not talking about the practical things now, like the interruptions and having to hide shoes, but the way Archie curls up between us on the sofa; the way he excitedly greets us both; simply the way he looks at us. Yes, we are wrapped round his little paw.

Archie loves us unconditionally. It's a good day for him simply because we're with him. We're his world. A dog has only basic requirements: food, water, a walk and some playtime, and of course, love.

Archie's my biggest fan, and I love him to bits. All the time we've spent together, the things we've done … I'm very lucky to have him – he's brought so much joy to my life.

If you have a bad day, think of the adult dog – how you want your dog to be in the future. The hard work is worth it. No-one else will ever love you the way your dog loves you. Enjoy your puppy!

Love from Helen and Archie x

Our trainer said that whilst we were getting to know Archie, Archie was busy compiling a big book on us! I often wonder what his book would read like. Here are some excerpts:

If I pick up something belonging to Mum or Dad, I can guarantee they will stop whatever they're doing and come after me. Then it's playtime – result!

If I run away when Dad gets my harness out, he'll chase me. It's a great game.

I'll never understand why Mum puts a jacket on me when it's raining. I love getting wet.

I LOVE LOVE LOVE fox poo and I wish Mum and Dad wouldn't wash it off. It's a shame they don't make fox poo scented shampoo. It'd be a winner, I'm sure.

Why do Mum and Dad try to get things out of my mouth? The brown stuff is really tasty. They should try it.

Mum and Dad seem to get all excited when I start digging in the garden. That means I should dig more often, right?

If I hang around the kitchen long enough, Mum almost always gives me an extra titbit. She talks to me a lot. I don't understand most of it, but I do like hearing her voice.

When Mum and Dad are cuddling up on the sofa, I jump on them and squeeze in between them. They always make room for me.

The trainer, by the way, told us that Archie was going to be an absolute delight; she was right – he is!

Here are some of my favourite pictures of Archie, which were taken over a period of 18 months (apart from the last photograph which shows Archie as he is now aged 2). If you would like to see a colour version of this collage, please go to: *http://helenlibbywriter.blogspot.com/p/a.html*

Photographs © Helen Edwards and Simon Edwards

Acknowledgements

I'd like to thank the key people who've helped us with Archie along the way; Evelyn, our dog trainer (Fun Way Dog Training); the team at the Willow Veterinary Centre in Newport Pagnell; Paula, Andy and Tilly (Tilly's PawPals) – we miss you.

In terms of getting this book together I'd like to thank Anne Hamilton of WriteRight Editing, who did a developmental edit and helped to shape the book to what it is today. Thanks for all your advice and encouragement. And to my husband, Simon, for being my sounding board – thank you x.

About the Author

Helen was born in North Wales and she currently lives in Shropshire with her husband, Simon, and her Zuchon dog, Archie. She has always loved writing, ever since she wrote a short story collection in the style of Enid Blyton when she was 12.

Helen also writes novelettes under the pseudonym of Helen Libby – all of which can be found on Amazon. She loves the Scottish Highlands, crisps, and anything sparkly. Find out more about both Helen and Archie at:

Blog: www.helenlibbywriter.blogspot.com

Facebook: www.facebook.com/ArchieZuchon

Instagram: @helibedw

Twitter: @helibedw

17455780R00026

Printed in Great Britain
by Amazon